TABATHA PITTMAN

Magnetic Woman

21 DAYS TO REGAIN YOUR POWER

21 Days To Regain Your Power

Magnetic Woman:

21 Days to Regain

Your Power

Tabatha Pittman

Email requests to info@TabathaPittman.com.
Ordering Information:
Quantity sales. Special discounts are available on quantity
purchases by corporations, associations, and others. For details,
contact the publisher at the email address above.
Published by Tabatha Pittman
Printed in USA
First Printing, 2020
ISBN: 97817335657288
ISBN-13: 97817335657288

9781735657288

DEDICATION

To every woman who is a friend, family and sister in the family of Christ, that has pushed me to become a better version of me, I sincerely thank you. To my children Amare, Samuel & Ashe, I thank you for teaching me many of the principles that will be shared throughout this book. Asking me "Who, What, When Where, Why and How?" I can honestly say that having you as my mirror and mini recorders is what I love most about being a mother. To my wonderful husband Samuel, there are not enough adjectives and adverbs that can describe what I feel for you. Your faithfulness, your dedication and your support have helped push me to the woman that I am today. All I can say is, "I LOVE YOU" for believing in and journeying with me to become what God called me to be a Magnetic Woman.

TABLE OF CONTENTS

Introduction

The Magnetic Woman speaks to self-confidence,

self-esteem, femininity, motherhood, wife life, and

the anointing that makes the difference to do it All.

I wrote this book to motivate a pursuit of excellence

in every Woman, to apply life's lessons to produce

growth and change in your Christian journey.

Proverbs 31, this is the ultimate woman. We call her

a woman of excellence; some texts call her a

virtuous woman. Today, in the 21st century, I

propose we call her the "Magnetic Woman." You

are a magnetic woman. You may say: how can we

live up to everything this woman was, even today?

I want to be clear, when I say Magnetic what I mean

is that although I am taking a cultural term does not

mean I agree with what culture says or defines it as.
I am taking the word Magnetic and just like God- I
am redeeming the word. When I say "Magnetic" I
do not mean the world's way, or the universe way,
or society's way. When I say "Magnetic" I mean
Christ's way! I am saying the Magnetic Woman is a
woman who is confident inside out, who embraces
every challenge in her career, business, home, and
marriage. She looks to Jesus, from whence her help
comes to manifest every desire of her heart. She
submits to her husband, and yet she knows how to
lead and be assertive in business and career
ventures. She is loyal in her friendships and caring
for others. She is effective in all these facets

because her pursuit is to live, love, and lead like

Jesus.

Magnetic Woman Daily Declarations

I am a woman who fears the Lord

I am a Woman of Excellence

I am a Woman of Virtue

I rise early to pray over, protect, and provide for my family

I am trusted and I lack nothing

I do good, and not evil, to all those connected to me all the days of my life

I am a wailing woman who wins in every area, department, and category of my life

I consider the profit and returns on my investments

I sow wisely and obediently

I submit to the Holy Spirit to guide, teach, and counsel me as He hears from Jesus

I work diligently and the works of my hands are blessed

I walk in the overflow and give generously to those in need

I am a kingdom financier

I am not afraid for my household, we are covered by the blood of Jesus

I am clothed in royalty and fulfillment of prophecy

My husband is known because I am a virtuous
woman

I am clothed in honor and I rejoice for the future is
bright

I open my mouth wide and speak; wisdom, kindness
and love are forever on my lips

I watch over my household with the eyes of the
eagle,

I do not eat the bread of idleness, jealousy
covetousness, envy nor pride

My husband and children arise and call me blessed

My husband praises and adores me

Many have done well, but I exceed them all because of my seat in the Kingdom of God

I am a woman who fears the Lord

I am honored and blessed for my work in my home, business, and community

God has given me the fruit of my hands

I am a Magnetic Woman in Jesus name!

DAY 1

SILENCE THE BACKGROUND NOISE

Failure does not define you, only the Father does.

The things that you have ran from out of fear, do not

define you. The mistakes you have made along

life's way that have caused or brought you shame,

do not define you. Your regrets do not have

authority over you. Understand this, mistakes,

situations, failures, trials, tribulations only come to

make you stronger. Know that it is all a setup for

your success. You were created to dominate and

walk in dominion. Dominate your fears, mistakes,

and failures. Dominate the background noise of

yesterday and yesteryear. All these things work together for the good of those that love the Lord. You are not defined by those moments. Those moments are part of your make-up, but they are not your foundation.

God is your source. On Christ the solid rock you stand, all other ground is sinking sand. Storms may rage, winds may blow but you have seen it all before. It did not define you then, and it does not define you now.

You are truly God's masterpiece.

When you walk in the room heads turn and eyes light up!

Magnetic Woman

DAY 2

PRETTY, PRESENT, & PURPOSED

When you have the right things on the inside, God will make a way for you to overcome what is happening on the outside. You are valued, and precious in God's sight. Look in the mirror and let the reflection captivate you at the mighty works of God's hands- that is the beauty of you.

You are a matter of great importance. You are more than a pretty box with no presence. You have the right things on the inside: Perseverance, Endurance, Persistence, tenacity, and the fruits of the spirit (love, long suffering, joy, peace, kindness,

goodness, faithfulness, gentleness, and self-control).
The Fruit of the Spirit yields a life of liberty.

You are mature, not as related to your age, but in how you carry your gifts, blessings, and assets. You understand that every gift you have is because God gave it to you. For that, all glory and honor belong to Him. He gives to you because you are a cheerful giver. He trusts you because you are a good steward. When you walk in the room you give life, and impact people's lives to push toward their purpose.

You are truly God's masterpiece.
When you walk in the room heads turn and eyes light up!
Magnetic Woman

Confidently Speaking:

Unforgiveness = Baggage! Let it go!

Forgiveness= Freedom!

You Choose

~Tabatha Pittman

DAY 3

DELIGHTFUL DIAMONDS

Beautiful, rare & cherished, you are a diamond.

Diamonds, like you, have characteristics that make

them highly sought after, valuable, and significant

to all blessed to have them. You are resilient, in that

you have the proven capacity to recover quickly

from difficulty. There is a toughness about you- not

in physical bulk or manliness but, inner strength.

You have been exposed to tremendous heat and

tried by the fires of life, society, and self. You have

withstood the cares and pressures of this world: real,

perceived, and discerned. Pressures that were meant

to break you. But God said, "Not so. Not You. Not today, Not ever." You might bend but, I decree and declare you will not break. You will bow for everyday is a grand finale where you receive a standing ovation for doing what you were uniquely designed to do- Be Magnetically You!

The jeweler will tell you it is all about the 4 C's: carat, cut, color, and clarity, which dictate the value and worth of each diamond. Behold the 5 C's of the Magnetic Woman in your mirror, a diamond in Gods' eyes has Cut, Color, Clarity, Carat and Christ.

A well-cut diamond will increase light return, adding to the diamond's sparkle. Some of those cuts were deep and left scars that you could not see at the time were meant to help you emit and transmit light to others. The cuts gave you style, pizazz, and character. These cuts helped to shape you not just princess, radiant, oval or marquise. You see God is a creative genius, the best gemologist known to man. He knows that the cut is critical, in such he did not spare any expense placing strategic cuts to get the best bling, brilliance and fire for you. You have always known you were cut from a different cloth, not because of where you are from, how much you have or who you were born to, but because you are an excellent quality. You are a cut above the rest.

When it comes to diamonds, the most valuable ones

are the ones within the white range because they

radiate every color of light. The color white

represents the purity that you possess, no matter

your skin tone. Your color and your fluorescence

(how a diamond behaves under ultraviolet light -that

makes white things appear even whiter) are always

turned to reverence God. When under the light you

behave in a way that entreats, pleases, and attracts

the favor of God. You walk in the victory that is

within from the beginning of the foundation of the

world.

The clarity of a diamond is determined by the

amount and location of flaws, or blemishes, in the

diamond when viewed under 10 times

magnification. As such, your worship brings you

closer to the Father's heart. There are people you

may see in the spotlight and they have been

groomed, manicured, and perfected to the naked

eye. So that we are clear, a diamond can look

perfect on the outside but with further inspection

have numerous imperfections. You, however, have

chosen to embrace every flaw, to see the joy in the

scars that tell the story of how you got over. Got

over the cheating, divorce, the molestations, the

abandonment, the lies, the good, the bad and the

ugly. You are filled with the light that magnifies the

flaws so that people, who knew you from ten years

ago, recognize that you are different. Yeah, you are different!

You are a woman of excellence worth far more than rubies. Everyone wants to talk about how many carats, because they do not comprehend the weight of what you carry. Their eyes are not trained to distinguish the pain that brought the gain. Just because the diamond is heavier does not always mean it is larger or will look bigger. Like you, the physical dimensions of the diamond are affected by how it is proportioned. You do not wear a small shirt just because you are small on bottom. You wear the shirt that is proportioned to your bustline. The largest diamond ever discovered was 3,106 carats, called the Cullinan. Yet God, the Father, recognizes that you are more than your carat weight, as a diamond you are His Star of Africa.

God calls you His precious jewel. In Malachi 3:17 God declares, "'They shall be Mine,' says the Lord of hosts, 'On the day that I make them my jewels.'" God is referring to you because you fear Him and meditate on His name day and night. Your name is written in the Book of Remembrance. He wants you to bask in His love. He wants to possess you in an intimate, loving, and beautiful way.

No longer will you be called a "Diamond in the Rough." God is unveiling your exceptional characteristics and manifesting your potential.

Where many thought you were lacking God is revealing that, just as a diamond, you are being cut by the chisel of His hammer, purposefully polished and finessed by His hands. He sees you as the ultimate gift of His unfailing love. You are brilliantly bright and beautifully crafted. You are a diamond, whose quality and design by the Master surpasses the physical realm of this age as you sparkle and shine forever in His glory to reach your ultimate destiny.

You are truly God's masterpiece.

When you walk in the room heads turn and eyes light up,

Magnetic Woman

DAY 4

ANOINTED

You have the oil. In the natural oil is not meant to moisturize your hair; nor in the spiritual is it meant to give you shine. You have been graced to carry the oil of joy for every sorrow you have encountered and endured. You shine because of the anointing that has been poured upon you. You shine like new money because the oil sets you apart and aligns you to walk in victory. You carry life, and birth dreams, missions, and visions. You carry creativity. Your voice is an instrument of music, harmony, rhythm, crescendos, and tempos. You are a melody of tears and smiles, hugs, and kisses. Your life is a bestselling love story of comfort and

encouragement, underestimated overcoming,

uplifting, and encompassing from your hair to your

stare and everything you wear: You have the shine

of anointing. Goodness and mercy follow you

because of the oil on your life.

The anointing oil is what makes the difference. The

oil you carry is often imitated, spectated,

commentated, and even hated but never duplicated.

Why? Because, like the woman with the alabaster

box, that oil is priceless. You had to toil for the oil.

When the oil comes upon you, you become a new

woman. The oil is also a sign of God's power,

authority, and charisma. Walk in the power, speak

with authority, and own the charisma of God that is upon your life.

Like Esther you have gone through a cleansing and beautification with the oil. The oil symbolizes the prosperity, blessing, and stability that is upon your life. Sanctification is also a result of the oil because you have been set apart as a blessed woman for the use and Glory of God. You are called Queen, for such a time as this.

You are truly God's masterpiece.

When you walk in the room heads turn and eyes light up,

Magnetic Woman

He has the Master Plan. When it looks like a setback, know it is a setup for greater love in Him. God has promised that His love will never fail you.

~Tabatha Pittman

DAY 5

HANDLE YOUR BUSINESS

You are an official member of "Handle Your

Business Ministries." To get from wherever you are

to where you want to be, let me welcome you to

"Handle Your Business Ministries!" You are

encouraged to find your happiness and operate in

stealth mode because some things are meant to be

sold, not told. Where you teach to be taught, as the

Holy Spirit leads you. Where your focus is clear,

and your prayers are answered without delay. Why?

Because the prince of Persia must bow to our God

and get out of the way for you to be blessed. Where

we ask and receive, knock and doors are opened,

seek, and find every good and perfect gift from the Lord with your name on it. At "Handle Your Business Ministries" we do not just pray in the spirit we slay all day in the Holy Ghost. We keep our hand to the plow, pen, and whatever tools we have been gifted with to stack coins, increase clients, and capacity for Christ by faith. You handle your business with sophistication, give your all, highest and best, study hard to turn tassels and pass every test. Here at "Handle Your Business Ministries" you are not comparing yourself to your neighbor's progress, because you have your own race to run. We pray, lift them, and lend a helping hand because we owe nothing but to love and understand. At "Handle Your Business Ministries" we have compassion for our fellow man and woman because we know what it is like to have and not have, to abase and abound. We have seen good and bad. We encourage one another to keep running toward your goal, not looking to the left or the right. At "Handle Your Business Ministries our first priority is to point all to the cross as we lift Jesus Christ.

You are truly God's masterpiece.

When you walk in the room heads turn and eyes light up,

Magnetic Woman

"Do Not Settle for Good,

Choose to Be Great.

Extraordinary People

Do Extraordinary Things!"

~Tabatha Pittman

DAY 6

EYES TO SEE

You are valuable. God sees it, and others see it. But the question is, do you see? You bring value to every room you walk in. Every person blessed to be connected to you is a benefactor of the value you bring.

When I was a younger woman, I struggled in a relationship where I was not valued. Elder Qualls, a Titus 2 woman, said to me: "Ask God to show you the Tabatha that He sees." It opened my eyes to be everything He called me to be. Today I implore you to do the same. I want you to see the woman God sees. He Is El Roi, the God who sees, as he saw

Hagar in the Old Testament. He sees you as highly

favored. God sees you as empowered. God sees you

as His daughter and calls you Beautiful. God sees

you as successful. He sees you as a peacemaker,

blessed are the peacemakers. He sees you as the

remnant- because you are turned from sin and have

returned to worship before God in spirit and in truth.

He sees you from His heart, a father's heart.

You are truly God's masterpiece.

When you walk in the room heads turn and eyes

light up,

Magnetic Woman

DAY 7

DUNAMIS DIALECT

God loves that you walk out what you talk about, that your life is a living testimony of His Dunamis power. Dunamis is where we get the English word dynamite. There is nothing quite like the person whose word does not hold weight and whose apologies wax hollow. Their mouth proclaims one thing, but their actions do not line up. When this happens the reputation of such will proceed you.

You must understand that your word is your bond. The bond that helps people go from knowing you to liking you, to doing business with you- to building

Kingdom with you. Most importantly your words

are powerful. Proverbs 18:21 says, "Death and life

are in the power of the tongue." You have the ability

to create kingdoms or tear down nations with the

life altering power of your spoken words. We must

speak words about ourselves and others that are

affirming and full of the Words of God. When we

do so we also speak in love and have a special

connection to God. His word cannot return void. He

loves to hear us repeat and regurgitate His Word

back to Him. Therefore, in Job 22, God asked him

if he had commanded his morning? Because when

you decree and declare a thing you establish it in the

earth realm, and you put the Word of God on

assignment. God will do it for His Glory and His name sake.

Yes, you confident Magnetic woman, you are qualified by your consistency and the words of your mouth being acceptable in God's sight.

You are truly God's masterpiece.

When you walk in the room heads turn and eyes light up,

Magnetic Woman

You are the masterpiece in each day-

Think like it, Act like it and Achieve like it!

~Tabatha Pittman

DAY 8

THE GIFT TO RECEIVE

You are a giver and a receiver. God intended for them to be a couple. He never meant for it to be a situation where you are the only benefiting others. This is not a get rich triangle where everyone struggles but the person at the top. You were created to do more than just survive. You were meant to thrive. This requires that your emotional, spiritual and physical bank get out of the insufficient funds' status. Allow this be your supernatural overdraft protection, and prophetic warning to cut off the drainers.

You know that you are anointed to give, it is often
the receiving part where you struggle. Let me first
say it does not make you any less brilliant,
magnificent nor magnetic that you receive. The
Bible says all things good and perfect come from
God. May blessings and gifts flow to you because
you are such a cheerful giver. You give of your
time, love, affection, concerns and resources and it
will be returned to you 100-fold. My sister use that
receiving muscle to open your hand so God can
flow to you and through you. A closed mouth does
not get fed and a closed hand cannot release nor
receive. Receive what is yours: increase, favor,
overflow, elevation, promotion, priority, and
provision and so much more!

You are truly God's masterpiece.

 When you walk in the room heads turn and eyes

light up,

Magnetic Woman

"In Order to Slay,

You Must Pray & Obey!

(Obey being the operative word)"

DAY 9

EMPOWERED BY THE

PROMISE KEEPER

Today we stand on the promises of God. The

original, often imitated, never duplicated, way

maker, miracle worker and Promise Keeper. I want

to encourage you today to sit awhile and meditate

on the promises of God. Every word spoken in the

Bible is infallible and inspired by God. That is to

say, every promise is a prophecy into your life.

Every word, every promise is accurate, detailed and

contoured to your life. So long as you apply it, He

will perform it until the day of Jesus Christ. You are

anointed. You are powerful because greater is He

that is in you than he that is in the world. His

promises have the authority to transform you, daily.

If anyone wants you to soar higher in success, God

does. He promised in Psalm 121 that he will not

allow your foot to slip. He will protect from the sun

and provide for you in your time of need. He will

perform His word because His word cannot return

to Him void. He delights in you because of the

unique oil you carry. Because of the divine

assignment on your life, He will perform every

promise. His promises are yes and Amen

concerning you, beloved. God has decreed it, you

have believed it, and now the performance of all

that was promised is manifesting in your life. Why?

Because he loves you beyond your welfare and

wellbeing. He likes and enjoys you as The Father.

You are always on His mind. You are more than one

of a kind, you are one in a million.

You are truly God's masterpiece.

When you walk in the room heads turn and eyes

light up,

Magnetic Woman

DAY 10

TELL HIM ALL ABOUT IT

Have a little talk with Jesus, tell him all about it.

Whatever it is that you have been dealing with I

invite you to have a conversation with Abba Daddy,

Jesus the Son, and the Holy Spirit- who is our

comforter and teacher. Prayer is merely a talk with

God. Prayer is about setting your affections on

Christ Jesus. When we set our heart on Him, he can

deliver us from whatever ails us. Every struggle you

are up against Jesus has already experienced and

conquered it.

I plead with you today, do not allow your vision of

your current condition to hinder your position in

Christ. Instead, focus on giving God glory and He will change the trajectory of your story. Many women in the Bible tell the story of bareness or infertility, but God. He saw fit, by faith to change the position of Sarah, Hannah, and Ruth; and He will do the same for you. Take it to God in prayer-petition the throne of grace. I encourage you to put laser focus on God. His power is above all power. He can do anything but fail. You see, God wants to make a testimony out of your life.

You are truly God's masterpiece.

When you walk in the room heads turn and eyes light up.

Magnetic Woman

DAY 11

WOMAN OF EXCELLENCE

You do not walk, you strut. Sister strut in your God given authority. Every new day you begin let it be with authority because God has not given you the spirit of fear, but of love, power, and a sound mind. Another translation interprets sound mind as self-control or self-management. So, act like it, act like you have self-management. You laugh at your mistakes, obstacles, and interruptions because you have a great sense of humor. You make the choice not to worry about what you do not know, because you know the one who knows it all. The great I Am. You are committed to him and He is committed to you. You open your mouth in obedience and utter

deep wisdom that could only come from the Holy

Ghost; simply because you are being you. You

know that all knowledge belongs to God and all

ignorance does too. Mighty woman of excellence

bask in the joy of these facts.

You are truly God's masterpiece.

When you walk in the room heads turn and eyes

light up,

Magnetic Woman

Don't stay a caterpillar all your life- there's a great chance you'll get squashed. Find your metamorphosis- and become the beautiful Butterfly you've dreamed about and God wants you to be!

~Tabatha Pittman

DAY 12

BUTTERFLY

You have given your last and given your first to

people who did not recognize your worth. For some,

you have given up everything to be with that person;

made them your reason for breathing till you

realized they were siphoning your air. I came to

resuscitate every magnificently magnetic woman.

Give your best to God and people, in that order. As

you keep Him first you will spring forward in every

area with new blooms. Do you perceive it?

You have been holding on to people who are

weakening your focus and blurring your vision.

Stop giving to someone who will not reciprocate

what you so desperately want, and unashamedly
need. Know that people cannot give to you what
they do not have within. You cannot get blood from
a turnip. Accept them for who they are or choose to
let them go. As your Magnetic Woman Coach, I say
this with love: "If it is a man or a mate, we are not
in the make-a-man (family, fan, friends) business-
PERIOD."

Today I command you to come out of that cocoon.
Transformation is your portion. I speak to the
butterfly in you. Breakthrough. Spread your wings
and soar like the eagles, higher than ever before. I
pray these gems bless you to know your worth and
value as God sees you.

You are truly God's masterpiece.

When you walk in the room heads turn and eyes

light up,

Magnetic Woman

Stay focused and know that you serve the God who is able to do exceedingly and abundantly above all you can ask or think! AND He'll keep you in Perfect Peace if you keep your mind stayed on Him!

~Tabatha Pittman

DAY 13

S.H.O.W. U.P.

I came up with this acronym as I was sitting with

the Holy Spirit in prayer: He told me to:

S.H.O.W.U. P. It translates to Spiritually Healthy

Overcoming Women United for Purpose. Show up

wherever you go. It does not matter if it is on Zoom

or at the local Trader Joes- Show Up. Show up

smelling like and looking like you represent the

bride. The bride is known to be well groomed, hair

done, vehicle clean, signature perfume wafting in

the air because you have been there. Your presence

is known. You have an essence about you. You are

the aroma of Christ. You Show Up because you are

a beauty to behold. You are glamour that is more

than diamonds and pearls, or the glistening of silver

and gold. Glamour is God's girl who Shows Up in

heels or tennis shoes. You Show Up natural, relaxed

or weaved because it is not what is on the outside

that tells the story. It is your inner beauty that

radiates and reveals His Glory.

Your spiritual health is on fleek because you eat the

scrolls and study the word of God to show yourself

approved. You have overcome obstacles, turned

stumbling blocks into steppingstones. You are in

unity with your fellow sisters and brothers in Christ

because you know that your purpose is to have all

signs pointing to Him. He said in John 12:32, "If I

be lifted up, I will draw all men unto me." Keep

lifting your hands and keep giving Him glory,

honor, and praise; and continue to S.H.O.W.U.P!

You are truly God's masterpiece.

When you walk in the room heads turn and eyes

light up,

Magnetic Woman

DAY 14

WITH LOVING KINDNESS

God wants you, as a Magnetic Woman, to extend

grace in your interaction and affairs with others.

You are to be mindful of being a re-presentation of

Christ in the earth realm. Know that it is not just

what you say but how you say it. Colossians 4:6

says, "Let your speech always be gracious, seasoned

with salt, so that you may know how you ought to

answer each person." When my children are

whining, I can choose to handle it with love or

frustration. I can tell them to stop acting like babies-

the flies to vinegar approach. Or I can address it

with loving kindness and nurturing saying: please

show me how a seven year old behaves. Likewise,

we can choose to confront or carefront. Confront is

defined as to meet face to face with hostile or

argumentative intent. Following that definition of

confront, as a Magnetic Woman, is like waving a

red flag in front of a bull and expecting it "not" to

charge. It will not yield a favorable result.

I present the alternative of *carefront*- that is to

approach every situation with care and compassion

for humanity as Christians. Putting this principle

into practice will almost always attract more bees

with honey. We know that the power of life and

death is in the tongue. Proverbs 16:24 also teaches

that, "Gracious words are like a honeycomb,

sweetness to the soul and health to the body."

You are truly God's masterpiece.

When you walk in the room heads turn and eyes

light up,

Magnetic Woman

DAY 15

QUEENDOM

I have a couple of questions for you today. I want to know:

1. What kind of Queen are you?

2. Are you using your platform to bring God Glory?

The book of Esther speaks of Queen Vashti and then her successor Queen Esther. Vashti was a leader of the women. Esther 1:17 says, "For the queen's conduct will become known to all the women, and so they will despise their husbands and say, 'King Xerxes commanded Queen Vashti to be brought before him, but she would not come.' When God has called you to a person, place, or thing it is important that you obey the Holy Spirit and the strategy he provides. Vashti is now in a dangerous place as her reputation throughout history and the word of God speaks for her. Due to disobedience, to her husband, she is replaced with a newer upgraded version. It is important that you use your platform for God's glory. Honoring your spouse is using your platform to give God Glory.

Esther on the other hand was a woman of influence, wisdom, and was led by the Holy Spirit. She found favor with eunuchs assigned to care for her. Hegai, who oversaw the harem, helped Esther gain the attention of King Ahasuerushad. She exercised wisdom in how to use her platform as a young Hebrew woman in the face of Persia. She used her platform productively and Godly. I do not care what your job is from mommy to pastor, from teacher to CEO to spouse, God has given you a platform. Finally, whether Esther knew it or not, she was being led by the Spirit of the Lord. Romans 8:14 says, "For all those who are led by God's spirit, these are God's sons." One of the greatest gifts God offers us is the privilege of being led by the Spirit of God. As children of God, we can expect to be led by the Holy Spirit which will provide us with the wisdom of God to make the right decisions. Your ability to tap into your calling is much easier when you make decisions based on the leading and

guiding of the Holy Spirit. This wisdom will allow

you to make decisions today based on knowing

what will happen tomorrow.

You are truly God's masterpiece.

When you walk in the room heads turn and eyes

light up,

Magnetic Woman

Be observant: Behaviors tell powerful stories, provide guidance and warning, instruction, and wisdom. Keep watching.

~Tabatha Pittman

DAY 16

CONFIDENTLY SPEAKING

Confidence: I want to make this abundantly clear; I am not talking about arrogance. We all know someone who thinks that she is too good for everyone else, men and women alike. By contrast, there are a few things that are more magnetic than a woman who is self-assured, one who can enter a room with a mixture of confidence and grace that communicates strength and elegance. A magnetic woman radiates confidence when she knows her worth; not the value of your car, your purse or your shoes. There is a difference in the value of an object and knowing your worth as a woman. The value is an agreed upon price that someone is willing to pay. Your self-worth is where you hold yourself in high esteem that agrees with what God says you are. You are rooted and grounded in the Word of God and working out your salvation daily. High self-esteem equips you with the skills to identify what you want and what you deserve to have in life and relationships. You are worthy of love and you are lovable, not because of what any man, woman boy or girl thinks but because of what you believe: God so loved You that He gave His only begotten son (John 3:16).

Actions speak louder than words. A magnetic woman does not talk about how great she is; rather, she lives a life that is a standard of excellence and gratitude. Let your life be a motion picture, of all the wondrous things God is doing, the leaps and bounds you have been able to accomplish with His divine plan in place.

It is not trying to be perfect for a person. As Felix Anderson would say, "perfection is the enemy of success." Confidence is not portraying entitlement or being overly assertive. As a magnetic woman confidence is simply owning who you are, having self-respect and employing the qualities that make you, You.

You are truly God's masterpiece.

When you walk in the room heads turn and eyes

light up,

Magnetic Woman

DAY 17

ROYALTY

Authenticity: When you admire the finest qualities

in other women, it is respectful and even thoughtful.

However, when you want to be that other woman it

detracts from the genuine you. As magnetic women,

we are original in our personality and perspective.

These qualities are refreshing and attractive. A

magnetic woman is a woman of royalty who knows

her sense of self, beauty, style, ideas, ambition, and

humility can attract the favor of God and man.

What kind of royalty are you? Today my

assignment from the Lord is to help you recognize

Real. We are going to separate the chickens from

the eagles. I know this may make some clutch your

pearls that I should even ask or compare. These are

both birds. They both have feathers and wings, and

they are in the same family, but there is a difference.

The chicken lives on the ground in that dusty

barnyard, scratching and clawing for food. The

chicken lives its life looking down at the ground.

The eagle is set apart on high and can canvas the

landscape for food. The biggest difference is how

they see themselves. That chicken, no matter where

you put it, will never fly. I want to let you know

You have wings and baby your wings are meant to

soar like eagles! Isaiah 40:31 tells us:

"but those who hope in the Lord will renew their strength. They will soar on wings like eagles; they will run and not grow weary; they will walk and not faint."

I must warn you that crows also soar! So, don't think you have it together on your own accord because that defines the "crow" mentality. I know we live in a "me, me, me" society, but we cannot do this alone. We have all fallen short of the glory of God according to Romans 3. We cannot do this without Jesus and each other. So, let me just fix your crown, Queen. It is ok to help each other out. We must humble ourselves and be able to help one another, with love. Sometimes that is a word of encouragement, sometimes a hug, or just a smile to brighten someone's day. Most of all we do not have to compete with each: Your beauty does not dim

mine- and me shining the light on you does not

make me shine any less.

You are truly God's masterpiece.

When you walk in the room heads turn and eyes

light up,

Magnetic Woman

DAY 18

FOR SUCH A TIME AS THIS

Queen Esther was a great and courageous leader.

She was extremely blessed to have several different

types of mentoring influences in her life. A mentor

is a person who provides resources for us that we do

not have on our own. I know, I know you "think"

you know everything. Let me tell you, the more I

learn the more I am flabbergasted at just how much

I do not know. And for that I thank God for

surrounding me with mentors. Esther had mentors,

plural. It may not be plain to the naked eye but if I

can invite you to put on your faith colored lenses,

we can follow her story a bit closer. Her first mentor

was Mordecai, her cousin who took her in after her parents died. We do not know what happened to her parents but what we do know is that a family member stepped up and stepped in. Perhaps you have had family step in or maybe you have been that village that it takes assuming the role of mama, daddy, friend, confidant, or mentor. Thank you, Jesus, for folks stepping up and stepping in!

Mordecai did not just turn her over to the king's court, he walked by the palace daily to get a status or an update on how she was doing. He was a spiritual advisor, as well. He told her not to reveal her nationality, you know that she was Jewish. The same mentors, aunts, uncles, grannies and nana's are going to call you and check up on you; no matter

your age because they love you. If you do not have

a mentor now is the time to get one.

Now, there is one more mentor that Esther had that

is essential to her Queendom. Mentors can also

come in the form of coaches and teachers. Ch 2:15

tells us that Esther had Hegai to train her for the role

she was to perform. Hegai was the king's eunuch, a

position given to watch over the harem of women to

be presented to the king. When the king's order and

edict had been proclaimed, many girls were brought

to the citadel of Susa and put under the care of

Hegai. Esther also was taken to the king's palace

and entrusted to Hegai. The girl pleased him and

won his favor. Immediately he provided her with her beauty treatments and special food. He assigned to her seven maids selected from the king's palace and moved her and her maids into the best place in the harem. You see when you link up with a mentor/teacher/coach you get a sponsor to be at the table, not just an invitation to the party. You get someone who sees the best in you and will hold you in high esteem, hold you up in prayer, be an accountability partner, teacher, friend, and spiritual advisor providing Biblical wisdom and sound counsel. If you do not have a mentor, get one, or better yet be a mentor because there are a lot of folks young and old yearning for this relationship. Let me offer and be the first to say, "I am available to you. Please reach out. I'd love to mentor or coach you."

> Phil 2: 1 Therefore, if you have any encouragement from being united with Christ, if any comfort from his love, if any common sharing in the Spirit, if any tenderness and compassion, 2 then make my joy complete by being like-minded, having the same love, being one in spirit and of one mind. 3 Do nothing out of selfish ambition or vain conceit. Rather, in humility value others above yourselves, 4 not looking to your own interests but each of you to the interests of the others.
>
> 5 In your relationships with one another, have the same mindset as Christ Jesus:
>
> 6 Who, being in very nature[a] God,

did not consider equality with God

something to be used to his own advantage;

7 rather, he made himself nothing

   by taking the very nature[b] of a servant,

   being made in human likeness.

8 And being found in appearance as a man,

   he humbled himself

   by becoming obedient to death—

     even death on a cross!

9 Therefore God exalted him to the highest place

   and gave him the name that is above every name,

10 that at the name of Jesus every knee should bow,

in heaven and on earth and under the earth,

11 and every tongue acknowledge that Jesus
Christ is Lord, to the glory of God the Father.

You are truly God's masterpiece.

When you walk in the room heads turn and eyes

light up,

Magnetic Woman

Thank you, Jesus, for loving me through my

good and my bad; For not erasing my future

because of my past. Nobody but JESUS can love

me this way!

~Tabatha Pittman

DAY 19

BY FAITH

Now faith is the substance of things hoped for the evidence of things not seen. Some call it optimism. Some call it positivity. I call it hope beyond hope. I call it trusting in the one who holds my future. Even when I cannot see through the fog of life, He gives Holy Ghost insight. He gives perfect vision, beyond my human eyes, and makes every provision. Then gives me the confidence to chase that vision to fruition. That is the gift of faith.

What someone says is an affirmation, I call it a declaration because God said I could command my morning. I continue to speak and call a thing that is not, as though it were. They speak to the universe; I serve The One who created the universe, hung the stars in the sky and put the planets in orbit. He is the bright and morning star!

He created everything, so He can do anything! Yes even "that thing" you have been dreaming of: He can save your family, restore your marriage, heal your body, give fertility in barrenness. The faith that provides when the bank says different, when the dealership cannot, HE WILL kind of faith. When the test is tough, Jesus gives you the Word kind of faith to pass with an Overcomer's testimony.

You are truly God's masterpiece.

When you walk in the room heads turn and eyes

light up,

Magnetic Woman

DAY 20

EMOTIONAL INTELLIGENCE

Your emotional health is vital to your success. As a woman we can be very in tune with our emotions, but it is more important that we have emotional intelligence. You may have heard this called "being in touch with your feelings or women's intuition."

What is emotional intelligence, or EI? The psychological perspective is that you can recognize, perceive, and express; as well as assimilate emotions in thought and understand emotions in self and others. From a Biblical perspective emotional intelligence is the display and activation of the

Fruits of the Spirit, in a psychological way. As
Christians, we can quote verses, and scriptures yet
lack application because we are emotionally
unhealthy. That is, we need to better name,
recognize and manage our feelings.

I recall an encounter where a client of mine was
having a hard time dealing with an overbearing
mother who needed her physical assistance. She told
me she felt broken by their relationship. I
encouraged her to acknowledge the feeling but not
to dwell on it nor engage it, but to keep pressing
toward the mark and to utilize her emotional
intelligence and self-awareness.

Additionally, we must identify with and have active compassion for our fellow brothers and sisters. The Bible says they will know us by the love we have one for another. You can do this by initiating and maintaining close and meaningful relationships. When you apply Emotional Intelligence, you give yourself permission to break free from self-destructive patterns that may have worked in the past; maybe they even worked for mama, aunties, sisters and friends. But when you know better you do better. Emotional intelligence acknowledges how the past has impacted the present and desires to push forward with corrective action to build a better future. However, to do this we must accurately assess our strengths, limits, and weaknesses. In so doing we learn the capacity to resolve conflicts

maturely. Again, *carefront versus confront.*

Carefront is to have appropriate "you have an ult

with your brother" dialogue to approach and resolve

a situation. This is not an all-encompassing

definition, but I believe as Magnetic Women there is

a level of excellence in Emotional Intelligence that

we must maintain no matter our position, the

degrees on the wall or commas in your bank

account. We show-up as fierce and fabulous, sweet,

and saved by exercising emotional intelligence, also

known as wisdom.

I want you to know that your feelings have nothing

to do with your purpose. You must do what you are

assigned to do and there will be times when the only way you can navigate the rivers is to operate in supernatural Emotional Intelligence.

You are truly God's masterpiece.

When you walk in the room heads turn and eyes light up,

Magnetic Woman

"God is transforming You from

Broken to Wholeness."

~Tabatha Pittman

DAY 21

ITS SHOWTIME!

You are a star, and it is ShowTime. You are going to Show Up and trust God for the greatness that is upon you. He wants His highest and Best for you in every step as you walk in the room.

We have talked about Showing Up, now it's time for God to Show Out on your behalf cause its ShowTime! Genesis 15: 1-5, Here we see Abraham and Abba Daddy having a conversation, and Abraham is complaining that he had not had children yet. Back then a patriarch would be one that would have a large family. He even thought he would have to make one of his servants his heir.

Verse 5 says: Then he, being God, brought him,

Abraham, outside and said, "look now toward

heaven, and count the stars if you are able to

number them." And He said to him, "So shall your

descendants be." It is Bigger than you. Maybe you

are on the fence deciding if you are going to follow

God or do it your way, again. You know you have a

call on your life, but it seems like all that you have

been through God cannot be in this with you. The

devil is a LIAR. All these things according to

Romans 8:28 are working together for your good.

That means the abortions, the mistreatment, the

abuse, people lying, using, and misusing your

kindness for weakness: it's all working for your

good! I decree and declare you shall not lose heart because you believe, and you are going to see the goodness of the Lord in the land of the living. I speak to the Magnetic Woman in you, I decree and declare that you will wait on the Lord and be of good courage. He will strengthen Your heart; wait I say on the Lord!

I urge you to GIVE IT ALL TO JESUS. Cast your cares on Him for He cares for you! There is nothing too hard for God. Did I say nothing? I meant nothing, nada, zero, zip, zilch! You are his beloved daughter, His prized possession. There is no mountain too high, no valley too low for God to move for you- His Magnetic Woman.

God desires you to live under an Open Heaven.

Under an open Heaven there are endless

possibilities. Your situation is meant to be a catalyst

to propel you forward. When you view your

situation from a head down perspective as the

chickens, you limit yourself. Instead look to the

heavens, as the eagle, mount up and let the winds of

the storm, the storms of life catapult you further and

higher than ever before.

Today, and from this day forward, I invite you to

see yourself differently- through the lens of the

Magnetic Woman. You are seated with Christ in

authority and power; making decisions, given

choices that effect change and impact destiny. You

are the overcomer who has allowed the pages of

your mind to explore the "more" of knowledge that

exceeds drips and flows to you and through you.

You are a leader and influencer. You are no longer

imagining; you write the vision, make it plain and

run with it. Focus is defined as the center of interest

or activity; it is what I like to call selective

attention- the ability to discern what not to give your

attention to. Focus is an underrated mental asset that

matters enormously for how we navigate this life in

Christ. Focus works much like a muscle: use it

poorly and it can wither; work it well and it grows.

Focus is what will allow God to develop your

character for where He is taking you. You must

maximize the time while you wait for prayers to

manifest; stay focused on Jesus. If you stay focused

you "ain't" got to get focused!

You are not just a hearer but a doer. No matter what

the "it" is, "Do It!" Create the design, finish the

dress, complete the certification. Push pass the now,

your future is at hand: Your hands! Look within to

the dreams of yesteryear and awaken the passion to

fulfill Your Purpose! The world is waiting on you to

take center stage and I am too.

You are truly God's masterpiece.

When you walk in the room heads turn and eyes

light up!

Magnetic Woman

<u>Closing Prayer</u>

Father, in the name of Jesus, I pray that you will bless every woman reading this. Touch them in a mighty way to turn from their own way and to enter the gate to their next level in you. Endow each woman with wisdom, supernatural discernment, and an increase in her faith to run her own race in Christ Jesus. Help us to submit to you, resist the devil and he will flee. Father, I ask in Jesus' name that you give each woman a powerful testimony to help another woman overcome by the blood of the lamb and the words of her testimony. Renew her strength so that she will mount up like eagles, to run and not grow weary, to walk and not faint. Create in us a clean heart to serve you and commit our steps and plans to you so you will establish and make us successful. Craft in us a sharp mind to be a solution to a problem and to see endless possibilities in you, Jesus. Help us to love one another and to extend the grace and mercy that you have extended toward us. May the peace that passes all understanding be her portion in all she says and does. May she rest in your unfailing love. Lord hold her close, restore and inspire with your sweet Holy Spirit to be all you have created her to be- the Magnetic Woman of Excellence. In Jesus' Holy name I ask and pray all these things!

Amen

About the Author

Tabatha Pittman is an intercessor and prayer warrior. She has answered the call on her life for the prophetic mantle and has a desire for the evangelistic objectives. Tabatha holds a Master's degree in Human Resources Management from Central Michigan University and a Bachelor's degree in Human Resources from Oakland University, as well as an Associate degree in Paralegal Studies from Columbus State. As a Human Resources Professional and Certified Professional Life Coach, she has a passion for professional and personal development, and has worked in multiple industries including automotive, logistics, technology, healthcare, and engineering.

Her goal, as a coach, is to align your passion with

your purpose, life objectives, and ultimately deliver

outcomes that matter to your life, relationships, and

career. She believes that accelerated readiness for

your future only happens with intention and

accountability. Tabatha gracefully combines

curiosity, compassion, and laser focus on ACTION

to yield results.

The Spirit of the Lord is upon me, because he hath

anointed me to preach the gospel to the poor; he

hath sent me to heal the brokenhearted, to preach

deliverance to the captives, and recovering of sight

to the blind, to set at liberty them that are bruised, to

preach the acceptable year of the Lord"   - Luke

4:18-19

Stay Connected

Instagram:The_Tabatha_Pittman

Facebook: TabathaPittmanlifecoach

Periscope: TabathaPittman

ShopMagneticWoman.Global

9781735657288

www.ingramcontent.com/pod-product-compliance
Lightning Source LLC
Chambersburg PA
CBHW072203090426
42740CB00012B/2375